Isabella Gibbons

Through Her Eyes

Isabella Gibbons

Through Her Eyes

by **Marc Boston**

Illustrated by
Araina Danielle Asher

MARC
BOSTON

JUJU SEEDS
www.jujuseeds.com

This is a sad but redemptive tale,
of how Isabella Gibbons struggled but did ultimately prevail.

Isabella's life has a mysterious start:
so many things are unknown about the first part.

What her early life was like, we don't know for sure,
but we have some idea of what she had to endure.

If we poke around the past, and peer through the haze,
we can piece together how she may have spent her days.

The children were little, but had to work just the same,
on land they would never be able to claim.

The harvests they collected were not their own,
and the back-breaking work made them tired to the bone.

There wasn't any crop they did not chop.
And they weren't allowed to rest until the man yelled, "Stop!"

Around the house, there was much work to be done,
cleaning and sewing until the evening sun.

They tended the kitchen garden, barefoot or in sandals.
They made household items like soaps and candles.

There was food to prepare and babies to rock.
They took care of the chickens and all the livestock.

If that's how hard children worked, I bet Isabella did, too.
Now you have an idea of what she might have gone through.

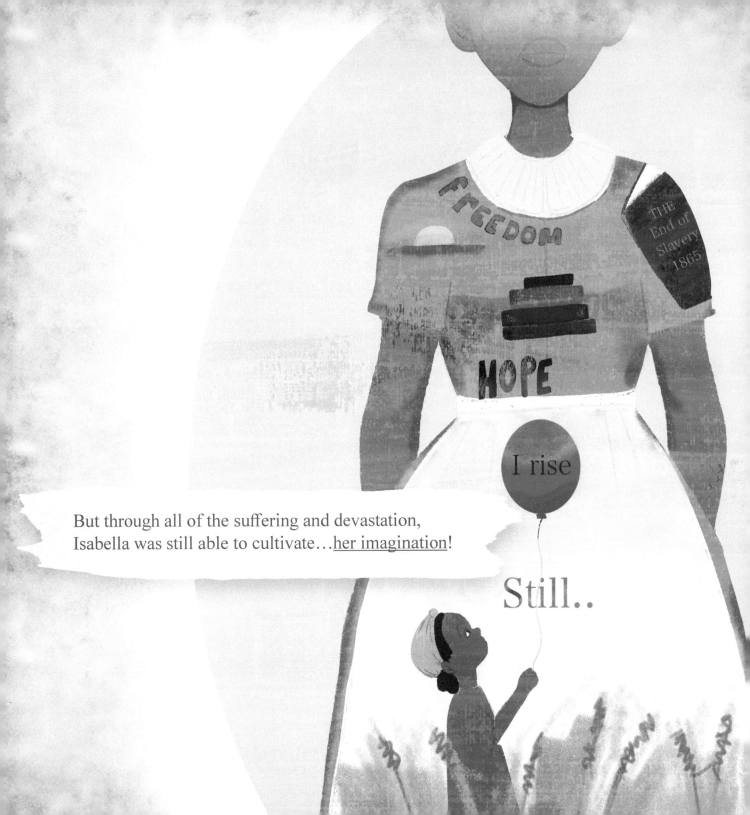

But through all of the suffering and devastation,
Isabella was still able to cultivate…<u>her imagination</u>!

Still..

She couldn't have had a bunch of material stuff.
But what she had inside would prove to be enough.

What you dream for yourself sets the foundation
of everything manifested in all of creation.

You might find it truly hard to believe
all the things Isabella was able to achieve.

Isabella lived in Virginia, where she worked as a cook.
She was determined to read and didn't care what it took.

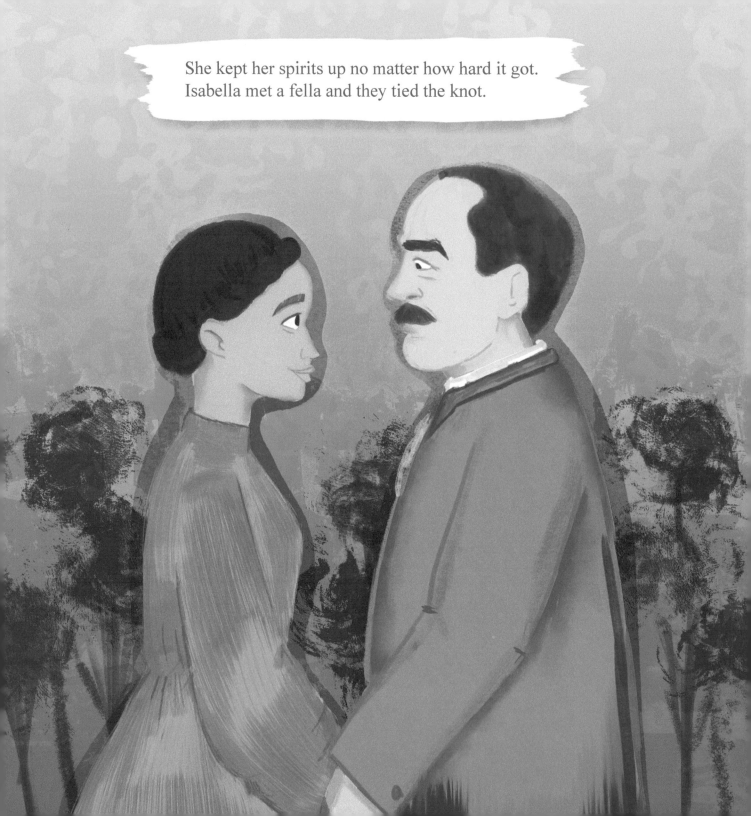

She kept her spirits up no matter how hard it got.
Isabella met a fella and they tied the knot.

Imagine her black hair full of bows and ribbons
on the day Isabella married Mr. William Gibbons.

The couple made a vow, so it was understood,
they'd make a better life for themselves as soon as they could.

When they had children, Isabella knew what to do.
The first chance she got, she taught them to read, too!

And when it came to teaching, she possessed something rare:
the courage to offer knowledge that some were unwilling to share.

Education is important and she lived by this rule.
So she provided guidance and began teaching school.

Of freedom and liberty she became a persistent seeker.
Isabella became a teacher and William Gibbons became a preacher.

It's clear they didn't allow their previous condition to deter them from the ultimate mission…

…And that mission is to be free.
This is what everyone wants to be!

Her sacrifice gives her the right to stand tall,
her eyes reverently placed on a memorial wall.

She's receiving her place of honor and praise.
Now none can escape her watchful gaze.

Those eyes remind us in the strongest way,
to turn grief from the past into change for today.

Gibbons Hall, University of Virginia

Through her eyes we saw the cruel world of the past,
choked by an "institution" that simply could not last.

Through her eyes we see the world with a clearer view,
we've come a long way but there's still more to do.

Through her eyes we'll _witness_ hates' eventual demise,
knowing **love is the truth** that never dies!

Look to Isabella for what it takes to rise,
and see the world in a new way...**_Through Isabella's Eyes_**.

GIBBONS

Afterword

By Dr. Jalane Schmidt

Isabella Gibbons (1836–1890)

Isabella Gibbons was enslaved at the University of Virginia (UVA), where her husband William was also enslaved. Because Isabella and William were "owned" by different professors, their family was split up between two Pavilion households on the UVA Lawn near the Rotunda.

Laws prohibited enslaved people from reading, but Isabella learned to read and write.

She was a mother and secretly educated her own 5 children. She wanted her son John to have a better life and allowed him to live in Charlottesville with Nancy West, a free African American woman who was a property owner. John West, as he came to be known, is the namesake of the Westhaven neighborhood and became the largest property owner in Albemarle County, Virginia.

After the Civil War ended in 1865, Isabella taught former slaves to read and write. In her teaching, she used Psalm 83, which *"I thought was suitable for the times."* The passage warns about enemies who would try to re-enslave the children of God.

In May 1867, Isabella earned a diploma from the New England Freedmen's Aid Society, an organization in Boston, Massachusetts, that became the benefactor of the Charlottesville Freedmen's School, which is now known as the Jefferson School.

Although she was not able to vote, Isabella was politically active and attended meetings of the Republican party, the "party of Lincoln."

She wrote a letter to the New England Freedmen's Aid Society, about the difficulties of life for formerly enslaved Black Southerners, part of which is inscribed on the Memorial for Enslaved Laborers at the University of Virginia, in Charlottesville:

CHARLOTTESVILLE, Va., March 29, 1867.

Can we forget the crack of the whip, cowhide, whipping-post, the auction-block, the hand-cuffs, the [manacles], the iron collar, the negro-trader tearing the young child from its mother's breast as a whelp from the lioness? Have we forgotten that by those horrible cruelties, hundreds of our race have been killed? No, we have not, nor ever will.

On the outward facing wall of the Memorial for Enslaved Laborers, Isabella's eyes are engraved as a tribute to her perseverance and firm resistance to enslavement.

Word Glossary

Redemptive - to make up for something, or to try to make something better.

Prevail - to be victorious; to get the win.

Devastation - great damage, sadness, or waste.

Manifested - to manifest something, is to make it appear.

Vow - to make a very big promise.

Cultivate - to develop, nurture, care for, or prepare something.

Possessed - to have, or to hold something.

Persistent - continuing to do something no matter what.

Deter - to try to keep someone from doing something.

Sacrifice - to give up something for the sake of something else more important than yourself.

Reverently - to show deep honor and respect.

Gaze - to fix your eyes on something; to stare.

Grief - deep sadness, or trouble.

Institution - an official organization of people having an important role in the lives of other people.

Demise - when something comes to an end.

For Marley, Delaney, and Journey.
Rach, thank you for all your continued support.
Thanks Ma, for always knowing.

Marc Boston is a father, husband and children's book author. He has three daughters and a beautiful wife who inspire him every day. His mission is to create stories that emphasize the importance of diversity and inclusion and reflect on topics surrounding definitions of family values and self-empowerment. He has written and published four other children's books: "*The Girl Who Carried Too Much Stuff,*" "*What About Me,*" "*Dad Is Acting Strange*" and "*A Promise to Grow.*" All are available at www.marcboston.com. You can follow his journey on www.facebook.com/marcgboston and www.instagram.com/marcgboston/

Araina Danielle Asher has loved drawing since she can remember. Her dad was an artist, so she grew up watching him paint and draw many amazing pieces. Araina grew up in Syracuse, NY, and attended the Art Institute of Seattle. She completed her coursework at Lasell College in Boston where she graduated with a B.S. in Fashion Design. Her favorite mediums to work in are watercolors, and pen and ink drawings. She happily resides in Syracuse, NY with her three kids. She draws and paints everyday no matter where she is or what she is doing. She always strives to live her best creative life! Visit www.arainadanielle.com to learn more.

Dedications

A very special thank you goes to the following creatives for coming together to bring this project to life:

Editors - C. Jumoke Boston and Jennifer L. Nelson
Illustrator - Araina Danielle Asher
Book Designer - mitchell&sennaar communications, inc.

We'd like to recognize and extend our heartfelt gratitude to the individuals and organizations who provided their invaluable contributions toward making this project a reality:

Dr. Jalane Schmidt
Dr. Claire Antone Payton
Dr. Jessica Kimpbell Johnson
University of Virginia's Memory Project
C. Jumoke Boston
Creative Consultant - Andrea Boston
Poet - Gary J. Boston
Artist - Erik McGowan

"Isabella Gibbons: Through Her Eyes" © 2022 Marc Boston
ISBN-13: 978-0-99868-99-1-3

Carolyn

J
U
M
O
K
E

BOSTON

Illustration by Erik McGowan

Sunsets
By
Gary J. Boston

I see you as the sun passes
Over the rim of the horizon,
as the last threads of sunlight kiss the tree tops.
I see you in the stars stretched
across the night sky, beautiful little
wonders shining just as brilliantly as you lived.
They're a reminder of how you told me to live.
To shine, despite the darkness.
To shine, because we have no choice but to.
I will see you always, in the big and
small moments of everyday, in every sky,
everywhere that touches
the well traveled places of my heart.
I will smile as we meet each other there.

In Loving Memory
C. Jumoke Boston

Sunrise - 8/9/47   Sunset - 12/22/21

Carolyn Jumoke Boston dedicated her life to cultivating and encouraging a life filled with joy, peace, and limitless abundance. A natural artist and former radio DJ, Jumoke established her own publishing company, Juju Seeds Media, where she edited manuscripts, and was instrumental in producing several works - including five illustrated children's books and two books of poetry written by her sons. She enjoyed photography, sculpting, drawing, music, traveling, and learning new skills to grow her freelance work as an editor and designer of the most beautiful publications. She was passionate about the safekeeping of children, and advocated for teens and children in the foster care system as an employee and volunteer for several organizations. Seeing a shortage of children's books that represent the perspective of people of color, she became passionate about publishing stories that emphasize the importance of diversity and inclusion as well as those that reflect on topics surrounding definitions of family values and self-empowerment. Jumoke was a vibrant woman with a great sense of humor who loved a good jazz show, an afternoon at the farmer's market, a family gathering, and a few hours spent watching the birds (especially cardinals) from her beloved front porch. We are saddened by her loss, but eternally grateful to have basked in her glow for the time she was here. Thank you Ma, until we meet again.

Printed in the USA
CPSIA information can be obtained
at www.ICGtesting.com
LVHW061119251123
764913LV00015B/74